30 days of Whole Foods Instant Pot Cookbook

The 50 Easiest + Fastest Whole Foods Instant Pot Recipes For Your 30-Day Challenge

by Emily Othan

Copyright © 2018
All rights reserved. No part of this book may be reproduced in any form without written permission from the publisher. This book may contain affiliate links, which helps support our work at no cost to you.

The health advice presented in this book is intended only as an informative resource guide to help you make informed decisions; it is not meant to replace the advice of a physician or to serve as a guide to self-treatment. Always seek competent medical help for any health condition or if there is any question about the appropriateness of a procedure or health recommendation.

Always follow safety and commonsense cooking protocol while using kitchen utensils, operating ovens, stoves, and appliances, and handling uncooked food. If children are assisting in the preparation of any recipe, they should always be supervised by an adult.

30 days of Whole Foods Instant Pot Cookbook

Want to help us spread the word about whole foods living?

Leave a review on Amazon!

A review is the best way to help spread the word about how easy it is to switch to a whole foods lifestyle, and hopefully it will help the next person find their way to healthier, easier whole foods Instant Pot meals, too!

To leave a review:

Type this URL into your browser: http://bit.ly/WholeInstantPot

OR

Google search "whole foods instant pot cookbook Emily Othan" and click the first Amazon link.

This should take you to the Amazon book page, where you can leave a review.

Thank you so much!

30 Days of Whole Foods Instant Pot Cookbook

The Easiest + Fastest Whole Foods Instant Pot Recipes For Your 30-Day Challenge

Table of Contents

Kid-Friendly	8
7 Ingredients or Less	9
20 Minutes or Less	9
Introduction	12
About the Whole Foods Instant Pot recipes	14
3 Hacks for Better Cooking in Your Instant Pot Electric Pressure Cooker	15
Chapter 1: An Overview of the 30 Day Whole Foods 30 Challenge	
What not to eat during the 30 day Whole Foods challenge	16
What to eat during the 30 day Whole Foods challenge	17
Sanity-saving Whole Foods substitutions for your 30 day challenge	18
Chapter 2: Understanding the Instant Pot electric pressure cooker	
Which Instant Pot model is right for you?	20
Which Instant Pot accessories are helpful?	20
How does the Instant Pot electric pressure cooker work?	22
Inside your Instant Pot pressure cooker	23
Understanding the Instant Pot buttons	24
Chapter 3: Whole Foods Egg Recipes for Your Instant Pot	26
Foolproof Hard-Boiled and Soft-Boiled Eggs	27
Ham and Broccoli Crustless Quiche	28
Chapter 4: Whole Foods Soup Recipes for Your Instant Pot	29
Creamy Butternut Squash and Sage Soup	30
Luscious and Light Carrot Soup	31

My Signature Lemon Chicken Soup	32
Fuss-Free French Onion Soup	33
Curried Pumpkin Soup	34
Creamy Broccoli and Apple Soup	35
Immune-Boost Chard and Sweet Potato Stew	36

Chapter 5: Whole Foods Chicken Recipes for Your Instant Pot — 37

One-Pot Thyme Chicken and Potatoes	38
Game-Time Buffalo Wings and Cauliflower	39
Fiesta Pulled Chicken Taco Bar	40
Chicken Marsala with Spaghetti Squash	41
Lemon Pepper Chicken with Baby Potatoes	42
Cranberry and Balsamic Chicken	43
The Easiest Indian Chicken Curry	44
Better-Than-Store-Bought Rotisserie Chicken	45
Our Go-To BBQ Drumsticks	46

Chapter 6: Whole Foods Seafood Recipes for Your Instant Pot — 47

Takeout Asian Salmon & Broccoli	48
Easy Lemon Garlic Salmon with Green Beans	49
Light and Fresh Mediterranean Cod	50
5-Minute Citrus Shrimp	51

Chapter 7: Whole Foods Pork Recipes for Your Instant Pot — 52

Sunday Favorite Pork Ragu	53
Pear Smothered Pork Chops	54
Artichoke and Lemon Pork Chops	55
Cuban Pulled Pork	56
6-Ingredient Kahlua Pork	57
Apple and Herb Pork Tenderloin	58
Cumin-Spiced Pulled Pork Carnitas	59

Chapter 8: Whole Foods Beef Recipes for Your Instant Pot — 60

Steak Fajita Stuffed Baked Potatoes	61

Guilt-Free Beef Goulash	62
Rosemary Braised Beef Short Ribs	63
One-Pot Beef, Potato, and Zucchini Stew	64
Simplest Beef Stroganoff	65
Mexican Meatloaf with Baby Potatoes	66
Lone Star State Beef Chili	67
Skinny Sloppy Joes	68
Chapter 9: Whole Foods Vegetable Recipes for Your Instant Pot	69
Perfect Potato and Cauliflower Mash	70
Sage and Garlic Spaghetti Squash	71
10-Minute Balsamic Roasted Beets	72
Flavor Bomb Asian Brussels Sprouts	73
Amazingly Adaptable Roasted Potatoes	74
Garlicky Mashed Potatoes	75
Easiest Baked Sweet Potatoes	76
Balsamic and Garlic Stewed Kale	77
Chapter 10: Whole Foods Compliant Sauces and Seasonings	78
Homemade BBQ Sauce	79
Whole Foods Compliant Lemon Pepper Seasoning	80
Whole Foods Compliant Taco Seasoning	81
Whole Foods Compliant Italian Seasoning	82
Whole Foods Compliant Indian Spice Mix	83
Cooking Times for the Instant Pot electric pressure cooker	84
Guidelines for Buying Organic Produce	87
Metric Conversion Charts	89
Helpful Resources for the 30 Day Whole Foods Challenge and Instant Pot	91
Did you find these recipes helpful?	92
Gift a book = give a meal!	93

Whole Foods Instant Pot Recipes by Category

Sometimes what I need most on busy nights is **the right recipe at the right time**. Don't you? Here are all the Whole Foods Instant Pot recipes in this book, grouped by their category, so that you can find a 20-minute recipe for when everyone's hangry, a 7-ingredient recipe for when you haven't had time to grocery shop, and a kid-friendly recipe for those extra cranky nights. I hope you find that the Instant Pot electric pressure cooker is just what you needed to rev up your 30 Day Whole Foods challenge!

You can find the page numbers for these recipes in the Table of Contents found in the previous pages.

Kid-Friendly Recipes
Foolproof Hard-Boiled and Soft-Boiled Eggs
Ham and Broccoli Crustless Quiche
Creamy Butternut Squash and Sage Soup
My Signature Lemon Chicken Soup
Curried Pumpkin Soup
Creamy Broccoli and Apple Soup
One-Pot Thyme Chicken and Potatoes
Game-Time Buffalo Wings and Cauliflower
Fiesta Pulled Chicken Taco Bar
Lemon Pepper Chicken with Baby Potatoes
Chicken Marsala with Spaghetti Squash
Better-Than-Store-Bought Rotisserie Chicken
Our Go-To BBQ Chicken Drumsticks
Takeout Asian Salmon and Broccoli
Easy Lemon Garlic Salmon and Potatoes
5-Minute Garlic Citrus Shrimp
Sunday Favorite Pork Ragu
Artichoke and Lemon Pork Chops
Cuban Pulled Pork
6-Ingredient Kahlua Pork
Apple and Herb Pork Tenderloin
Cumin-Spiced Pulled Pork Carnitas
Steak Fajita Stuffed Baked Potatoes
Guilt-Free Beef Goulash
One-Pot Beef, Potato, and Zucchini Stew
Simplest Beef Stroganoff
Mexican Meatloaf with Baby Potatoes
Lone Star State Beef Chili
Skinny Sloppy Joes
Perfect Potato and Cauliflower Mash
Amazingly Adaptable Roasted Potatoes
Garlicky Mashed Potatoes

Easiest Baked Sweet Potatoes
Homemade BBQ Sauce
Lemon Pepper Seasoning
Italian Seasoning
Indian Spice Mix
Taco Seasoning

7 Ingredients or Less Recipes
Foolproof Hard-Boiled and Soft-Boiled Eggs
Ham and Broccoli Crustless Quiche
Creamy Butternut Squash and Sage Soup
Fuss-Free French Onion Soup
Game-Time Buffalo Wings and Cauliflower
Fiesta Pulled Chicken Taco Bar
Lemon Pepper Chicken with Baby Potatoes
Better-Than-Store-Bought Rotisserie Chicken
Our Go-To BBQ Chicken Drumsticks
Easy Lemon Garlic Salmon with Green Beans
5-Minute Garlic Citrus Shrimp
Sunday Favorite Pork Ragu
Pear Smothered Pork Chops
Cuban Pulled Pork
6-Ingredient Kahlua Pork
Apple and Herb Pork Tenderloin
Rosemary Braised Beef Short Ribs
Perfect Potato and Cauliflower Mash
Sage and Garlic Spaghetti Squash
10-Minute Balsamic Roasted Beets
Amazingly Adaptable Roasted Potatoes
Garlicky Mashed Potatoes
Easiest Baked Sweet Potatoes
Balsamic and Garlic Stewed Kale
Lemon Pepper Seasoning
Italian Seasoning
Indian Spice Mix
Taco Seasoning

20 Minutes or Less Recipes
Foolproof Hard-Boiled and Soft-Boiled Eggs
Creamy Butternut Squash and Sage Soup
Luscious and Light Carrot Soup
Fuss-Free French Onion Soup
Creamy Broccoli and Apple Soup
Immune-Boost Chard and Sweet Potato Stew
One-Pot Thyme Chicken and Potatoes

Game-Time Buffalo Wings and Cauliflower
Fiesta Pulled Chicken Taco Bar
Cranberry and Balsamic Chicken
The Easiest Indian Chicken Curry
Our Go-To BBQ Chicken Drumsticks
Takeout Asian Salmon and Broccoli
Easy Lemon Garlic Salmon and Potatoes
Light and Fresh Mediterranean Cod
5-Minute Garlic Citrus Shrimp
Pear Smothered Pork Chops
Artichoke and Lemon Pork Chops
Simplest Beef Stroganoff
Skinny Sloppy Joes
Perfect Potato and Cauliflower Mash
Sage and Garlic Spaghetti Squash
10-Minute Balsamic Roasted Beets
Flavor Bomb Asian Brussels Sprouts
Amazingly Adaptable Roasted Potatoes
Garlicky Mashed Potatoes
Balsamic and Garlic Stewed Kale
Homemade BBQ Sauce
Lemon Pepper Seasoning
Taco Seasoning
Italian Seasoning
Indian Spice Mix

Introduction

I've never thought of myself as a dieter. (Says the woman writing a book on how to do a 30 day whole foods challenge—ha!)

But then I had twins, and life started to get even busier. Soon, I realized my jeans were a little tighter and my motivation a little lower each day. Just as bad, I felt SO tired all the time. It was difficult enough to get through my to-do list each day and take care of my family, and I just couldn't seem to find the time or energy to go to the gym.

Feeling depressed that my health was always being pushed to the backburner, I finally caved and bought *The Whole 30: The 30-Day Guide to Total Health and Food Freedom* by Melissa Hartwig and Dallas Hartwig.

I'd heard all about doing a 30 day whole foods challenge from friends and family for months. But when I realized that my friends—who were just as busy and stretched thin as I was—were suddenly healthier, thinner, and more energetic than I'd seen them in years, I realized that I needed to do whatever they were doing, and quick.

My husband and I decided to do a 30 day whole foods challenge together, **and it totally changed us**. We started thinking about food differently, and we couldn't believe how good eating grain-free, dairty-free whole foods way made us feel. We felt younger, stronger, and happier than we had in years.

But at around Day 15 in the 30-day challenge, we started to get burned out on cooking every night. On a diet plan like this, you eat only healthy, unprocessed whole foods, and so cooking at home is often the only option.

We loved that we were cooking and eating together as a family more, and our kids were already less stressed and more interested in what was going on in the kitchen. But we needed quicker and easier recipes. And on top of that, we needed them to be kid-friendly *and* whole foods challenge compliant. I was stumped.

Around that time, I received an Instant Pot electric pressure cooker as a gift from my mom, who is an incredible cook and obsessed with her Instant Pot. **That was a big breakthrough for us as a family:** the Instant Pot allowed us to finally spend less time in the kitchen, without having to sacrifice our weight loss goals.

Now, dinner at my house looks like this: I toss a few ingredients in the Instant Pot, set it to electric pressure cooking mode, then hang out in the living room, catching up with my husband or helping the kids with their homework. No more watching and stirring over the stove or peeking and prodding in the oven!

I hope you enjoy this collection of Whole Foods Instant Pot recipes as much as my family has. My wish is that this book makes you and your family healthier and happier, one meal at a time.

If you do find these Whole Foods Instant Pot recipes helpful, would you consider leaving a review on Amazon? It would mean so much to me and will hopefully help the next person find their way to an easier, healthier time in the kitchen! You can leave a review here: http://bit.ly/WholeInstantPot, which takes you directly to the Amazon page.

Thank you so much for purchasing this book, and happy cooking!

Emily

About the Whole Foods Instant Pot Recipes in this Book

The Whole Foods Instant Pot recipes in this book are designed with real families in mind: the kind who want to eat real, whole foods, but also need to keep dinner quick, easy, and affordable.

Within these pages you'll find my very favorite Whole Foods Instant Pot recipes. They're the keepers that I turn to again and again, and here's why I think you'll love them, too:

Each Whole Foods Instant Pot recipe aims for:

- **Easy-to-find, affordable ingredients:** You won't find any expensive or unpronounceable ingredients here. While there are a few keys items you'll want to buy when you stock your whole foods compliant pantry, I make sure they get used over and over in other recipes, so you're not stuck with an ingredient you'll never use again. (I hate that!)

- **Kid-friendly, adaptable recipes:** My kids are super picky eaters, so I always create recipes with them in mind. These Whole Foods Instant Pot recipes are as simple as they can be while still being flavorful. Even better, each recipe says whether it's especially kid-friendly. Where possible, I included suggestions for how to adapt the recipe for both adult and kid taste buds. Remember, these recipes are designed to serve as templates for everything that's possible with your Instant Pot, so never hesitate to skip or substitute flavoring ingredients like spices or sauces if your kiddos don't like them!

- **7 Ingredient or Less recipes:** If you're like me and don't want to spend tons of time pulling ingredients from cabinets and measuring them, these Whole Foods Instant Pot recipes are for you! The recipes will point out if it's a 7 Ingredient or Less recipe (not including salt and pepper, of course). That way, you can easily turn to these recipes on nights when you really want to keep things simple. (Helloooo, Wednesday night soccer practice.)

- **20 Minutes or Less recipes:** The beauty of the Instant Pot electric pressure cooker is that it's hands-free cooking, and it's incredibly fast. I've highlighted the recipes that are 20 Minutes or Less to cook once at pressure, so you can quickly turn to those when you have cranky kids or a hangry husband to feed. (Basically every night in my house…)

3 Hacks for Better Instant Pot Cooking

After experimenting with the Instant Pot electric pressure cooker for nearly a year, I've learned a few hacks that make the best use of this handy new appliance. I use these almost every single time I make a Whole Foods Instant Pot recipe, and they've saved me hundreds of hours in the kitchen, plus resulted in more flavorful meals.

1. Thicken the sauce, if you have the time.

Because the Instant Pot always needs to have about 1 cup of liquid in it for the food to steam correctly, you'll get delicious broths and sauces with nearly every meal.

But sometimes, you might find that you have too much liquid after cooking, and that it's a bit thin. Sauté setting: to the rescue! If I have time, I'll often remove the food from the Instant Pot, leaving the sauce, and then set the pot on high heat on the Sauté setting. You can let it cook down as much as you want, or add a thickener to make it more like a gravy. A great Whole Foods compliant thickener is arrowroot powder, which you can find online or at specialty food stores.

> **To make an arrowroot powder thickener:**
> Combine 1 teaspoon arrowroot powder + 1 tablespoon water.
> Slowly whisk into the liquid and allow to cook until thickened.

2. Use the pocket of time during pressure cooking to make a side.

When I first start looking for Instant Pot recipes, it seemed like many of them had you first cook the protein, then empty the pot and cook a vegetable side. Yikes—I don't have time for that! If you don't either, here's what I suggest: get your Instant Pot recipe locked and loaded, then use the time during pressure cooking to toss together quick roasted vegetables, spiralizer your zoodles, or microwave a few baked potatoes.

My favorite Whole Foods compliant side is a big tray of brussels sprouts, cauliflower, or broccoli, which I cook under the broiler instead of roasting, to save even more time.

> **To make quick and easy broiled vegetables:**
> Toss 1-inch pieces of any oven-friendly veg with olive oil, salt, and pepper.
> Place under the broiler until crispy, watching carefully so they don't burn.

3. Taste your food before serving and add more salt and pepper, if necessary.

We all like our food at different levels of saltiness and pepperiness, so please always take my measurements as a suggestion, not a rule! This is especially true of Instant Pot recipes, since you're often using broth as the steaming liquid. Different brands of broth have vastly different salt content, so if you're unsure how salty your broth might be, use less salt before pressure cooking. You can always add more salt and pepper once you open up the pot again!

Chapter 1: An Overview of the 30 Day Whole Foods Challenge

A 30 day Whole Foods challenge can mean many things, but most commonly it's considered to be a grain-free, dairy-free, legume-free diet that focuses on eating only natural, whole foods. You can do the diet for 30 days to reset your body, or you can stick with it indefinitely. At its core it is an elimination diet, meaning that it's designed to cut out foods that cause weight gain, decrease your energy, or which cause inflammation or food sensitivities in many people

Oftentimes, we *think* we have no problem eating certain foods, but we're usually too busy, too distracted, or too out-of-tune with our bodies to notice that they're making us feel bloated, tired, or just heavy-feeling. By seeing how we feel when we cut out those foods for 30 days, we can finally—usually for the first time in our lives—see how our bodies feel when we fill them only with real, nourishing food.

What Not to Eat During the 30 Day Whole Foods Challenge

Grains
   No pasta, bread, rice, corn, quinoa, barley, farro, wheat, and other grains.

Legumes
   No beans, peas, lentils, chickpeas, peanuts, soy in any form, and other legumes.

Dairy products
   No milk, cheese, yogurt, cream, butter and other dairy. Ghee (clarified butter) is compliant with most popular 30 day whole foods diets because it does not contain lactose.

Sugar
   No stevia, artificial sweeteners, honey, maple syrup, agave, and others. Only fruit or fruit juice is okay as a sweetener.

Alcohol
   No beer, wine, and liquor, either for drinking or cooking.

Additives
   No MSG, carrageenan, nitrates, and any other non-food ingredients.

What to Eat During the 30 Day Whole Foods Challenge

The great news is that there are so many foods you CAN eat during your 30 Day Whole Foods challenge, and once you start adjusting to this new way of eating and seeing how amazing it makes you feel, you won't want to go back to your carb-loading, sweet tooth ways.

You can eat as much as you want of these compliant foods:

Compliant Foods:
- Meat
- Poultry
- Seafood
- Vegetables
- Eggs
- Potatoes (Potatoes are compliant because they're a whole food, but fries, chips, and any other deep-fried potatoes are excluded because they are most often processed.)
- Fruit
- Nuts and seeds (excluding peanuts, which are a legume)
- Oils and ghee

The following are popular compliant ingredients:
- Almond flour
- Almond milk
- Arrowroot Powder
- Bacon
- Bean Sprouts
- Cacao
- Canola Oil
- Olive Oil
- Carob
- Chia
- Citric Acid
- Coconut Flour
- Coconut Water
- Coconut Aminos
- Coffee
- Dates
- Flax Seed
- Fruit Juice
- Green Beans
- Hemp Seeds
- Mustard
- Nutritional Yeast
- Sunflower Oil
- Snow Peas
- Tahini

Sanity-Saving Whole Foods Substitutions for Your 30-Day Challenge

While 30 days may seem like a long time to go without foods you're used to eating, once you get the hang of the substitutions, you'll see that you can still cook and enjoy many of your favorite recipes. With the right items in your Whole Foods compliant pantry, you'll quickly and easily be able to adapt your cooking to your healthy new life.

Instead of wheat flour, **use almond flour**.
> Use a quality brand like Bob's Red Mill, which you can find at http://bit.ly/bobsflour.

Instead of soy sauce, **use coconut aminos.**
> The Coconut Secret brand is compliant with most popular whole foods diets and can be found at http://bit.ly/coconutsecretaminos.

Instead of butter, **use ghee (also known as clarified butter).**
> I swear by the Trader Joe's brand, which you can also buy on Amazon at http://bit.ly/traderjoesghee.

Instead of regular barbeque sauce, **use Not Ketchup BBQ Sauce.**
> You can find it on Amazon at http://bit.ly/notketchupbbqsauce; it's one of the few Whole Foods compliant BBQ sauces. (Or make your own with the recipe in this book!)

Instead of milk, use **unsweetened original almond milk or unsweetened coconut milk.**
> Pacific is a popular almond milk brand and can be used in savory dishes. It can be found online here: http://bit.ly/pacificfoodsalmondmilk.
>
> Unsweetened coconut milk is best used in Indian or Asian dishes due to its coconut flavor. Thai Kitchen is a popular lectin-free brand and is available online at http://bit.ly/thaikitchencoconutmilk.

Instead of sugar, use 100% pure, unsweetened fruit juice.
> A Whole Foods compliant grape juice and cherry juice are helpful to have on hand for making fruit desserts. I like the one found here: http://bit.ly/GrapeJuice.
>
> You may also want to have date paste for sweetening dishes or making homemade BBQ sauce. Date paste is easier to find online than in stores—this is a favorite: http://bit.ly/NoSugarDatePaste.

Instead of cornstarch for thickening, use arrowroot powder.
> You can find it online at http://bit.ly/starwestarrowroot, and even though it can be a bit pricey, it lasts forever.

An important note on broth:

Because of how the Instant Pot pressure cooks, it typically requires about 1 cup of liquid in the pot. You'll see that many of the recipes in this book call for chicken or beef broth, but please keep in mind that the quality of your broth will heavily influence the flavor of the final dish.

Try Bone Broth by Kettle & Fire, available here: http://bit.ly/kettlefirebeefbonebroth, for a top-of-the-line, just-like-homemade flavor.

Or for a more affordable, yet still delicious, option, try Pacific's organic, free-range line, available at many grocery stores or online at http://bit.ly/pacificchickenbroth.

Chapter 2: Understanding the Instant Pot Electric Pressure Cooker

The Instant Pot is America's #1 bestselling electric pressure cooker for a reason: because it's so much more than just a pressure cooker! The Instant Pot is a first-of-its kind multi-cooker, which combines a slow cooker, pressure cooker, and rice cooker into one handy electric appliance. Even better, the Instant Pot has a sauté function which allows you to brown vegetables, sear meat, and easily build flavor right in the pot, unlike traditional slow cookers or pressure cookers.

Which Instant Pot model is right for you?

If you want all 9 settings:
  Get the Instant Pot DUO Plus 60 6 Quart 9-in-1 model here: http://bit.ly/instantpot9in1

If you cook for a crowd:
  Get the Instant Pot DUO80 7-in-1 in the 8 quart size here: http://bit.ly/instantpoteightqt

If you have a small kitchen:
  Get the Instant Pot DUO80 7-in1 in the 3 quart size here: http://bit.ly/instantpot3qt

If you're on a budget:
  Get the Instant Pot LUX60 V3 6-in-1 in the 6 quart size here: http://bit.ly/instantpot6qt

Which Instant Pot accessories are helpful?

While you don't need additional accessories to make any of the recipes in this book, you might find it helpful to have a few Instant Pot-friendly items to make things a little easier on yourself.

For steaming vegetables, seafood, or delicate cuts of meat:
  Instant Pot makes **a silicone steamer set,** available here,
  http://bit.ly/instantpotsteamerset, which makes it easier to use the Steam setting.

For easily removing the trivet or pot without burning yourself:
  Try Instant Pot's **silicone mini mitts**, which are practical, easy to store, and cute to boot! They can be found online here: http://bit.ly/instantpotminimitts

For storing leftovers in your pot in the refrigerator:
  You can get a **silicone lid cover** here: http://bit.ly/instantpotsiliconelid. It fits snugly over your pot, saving you clean-up time after dinner.

For doubling up on your pressure cooking:
  Get **an Instant Pot-approved back-up pot**, for those times when you want to cook recipes back-to-back in your pot without doing dishes in between. Available online at http://bit.ly/instantpotinnerpot.

For more Instant Pot recipes:

I love *The Essential Instant Pot Cookbook* by Coco Morante and *Dinner in an Instant* by Melissa Clark.

Not all the recipes are low calorie, but you'll find great inspiration and you can modify many of the recipes to fit your new low calorie lifestyle.

You can find the *The Essential Instant Pot Cookbook* here: http://bit.ly/essentialinstantpot

You can find *Dinner in an Instant* here: http://bit.ly/DinnerInAnInstant

How does the Instant Pot pressure cook?

You may be coming to the Instant Pot with preconceived notions of what a pressure cooker is. Maybe you've heard stories about pressure cookers overflowing or spraying food everywhere, or maybe you remember the old-fashioned pressure cookers that loudly (and annoyingly) whistled.

Forget all those ideas, because the Instant Pot is different. Because the Instant Pot is an *electric* pressure cooker that was specifically designed to be safer than stovetop pressure cookers, it has few of the issues of old-fashioned pressure cookers. But if you're like me and like to know how things work, you might be wondering how, exactly, the Instant Pot cooks food using the pressure cooking setting.

The Instant Pot electric pressure cooker program begins when you set the Pressure Release valve to "Sealing." From there, you select the program and set the desired time. The Instant Pot will give you 30-60 seconds to make your selections, then it will automatically initiate the program.

As the Instant Pot begins to build heat, the pressure increases in the pot and the boiling point of the water or liquid in the pot also increases. As more and more steam is generated, the pressure continues to increase inside the pot. The water begins to reach a very high temperature, yet the high pressure and the increased boiling point prevents the water from boiling or evaporating.

The high-heat, high-moisture environment of the Instant Pot means you get exceptionally quick cooking times and incredibly moist food. Even typically dry cuts of meat, such as boneless skinless chicken breasts come out juicy and moist in just a few minutes. This makes it almost impossible to overcook or dry out your food—and who doesn't want that?!

Inside Your Instant Pot Pressure Cooker

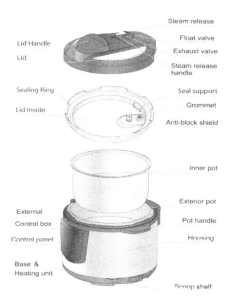

While other electric pressure cookers may have features that are different from the Instant Pot, almost all electric pressure cookers have several key parts:

Inner pot. Sometimes also referred to as the cooking pot. The inner pot is stainless steel, so it's easy to wash and can also be used to store leftovers in the refrigerator.

Heating element. The heating element is electric, meaning that you can plug in the pot and set it on your countertop, just like a slow cooker. This makes it perfect for small kitchens!

Sensors. The Instant Pot has several built-in pressure and temperature sensors that make it safer than a nonelectric pressure cooker. These sensors monitor the internal environment, maintain the desired cooking conditions, and help protect you from possible mishaps.

Locking mechanism. The Instant Pot has a sealing ring that creates a completely airtight chamber inside the pot so that steam can build up. Once you turn the pot lid to the Closed position, the vacuum seal is formed. The lid locks in place, so that you can't accidentally open the lid when the pot is at a high pressure.

Push down pressure release: The valves that are installed in the Instant Pot are designed with an innovative Anti-Block Shield that allows them to automatically react to changing conditions in the pot. The valves remain locked until the pressure goes beyond the specified threshold, at which point the valve pushes itself upward, slowly releasing the pressure and returning it to normal levels. These release valves are intelligently controlled with electronic sensors which automatically alter the settings depending on the type of food you're cooking.

Understanding the Instant Pot Buttons

The Instant Pot is preprogrammed with various cooking settings, so that you can quickly and easily select the cooking program that's right for each kind of food. The Instant Pot company has spent years assimilating data from hundreds of chefs all over the world to arrive at these pre-programmed times, so the settings have a high level of accuracy.

Of course, a setting like "Bean" will only work if you have the recommended quantity of beans and liquid in the pot, so it's important to follow an Instant Pot recipe rather than just guess at the setting. You can also find comprehensive cooking times for basic ingredients in the Cooking Times for the Instant Pot Electric Pressure Cooker chart at the back of this book.

The Instant Pot comes in many models and sizes, so you may not have these exact buttons. If not, don't worry: you can always use the Manual or Pressure Cook setting to replicate the same results produced by the other buttons.

Sauté: Use this to sauté vegetables, sear meat, simmer a soup, thicken a sauce, or otherwise cook food over high heat like you would on the stovetop. This setting should only be used with the lid removed. Many Instant Pot models include buttons that allow you to adjust the heat to Low, Normal, or High, just as you would on the stovetop.

Keep Warm/Cancel: Use this button to turn your pressure cooker off or reset the cooking program. You can also use it to keep food warm in the Instant Pot until you're ready to serve it.

Manual: This is your go-to button for setting a cooking program. The manual button lets you set any cooking time at any pressure level, so it's a good back-up if your Instant Pot doesn't have a specific program called for in a recipe.

Soup: This will set the program to pressure cook, and you can adjust the time to 30 minutes of cooking time (at normal); 40 minutes (at more); 20 minutes (at less).

Meat/Stew: This will set the program to pressure cook, and you can adjust the time to 35 minutes of cooking time (at normal); 45 minutes (at more); 20 minutes (at less).

Bean/Chili: This will set the program to pressure cook, and you can adjust the time to 30 minutes of cooking time (at normal); 40 minutes (at more); 25 minutes (at less).

Poultry: This will set the program to pressure cook, and you can adjust the time to 15 minutes of cooking time (at normal); 30 minutes (at more); 5 minutes (at less).

Rice: This is a fully automated mode which allows you to easily cook rice on low pressure. It will adjust the timer automatically, depending on the amount of water and rice present inside the inner cooking pot.

Multi-Grain: This will set the program to pressure cook, and you can adjust the time to 40 minutes of cooking time (at normal); 45 minutes (at more); 20 minutes (at less).

Porridge: This will set the program to pressure cook, and you can adjust the time to 20 minutes of cooking time (at normal); 30 minutes (at more); 15 minutes (at less).

Steam: This setting is useful for quickly steaming vegetables, seafood, or thin cuts of meats. It will set your pressure cooker to high pressure with 10 minutes of cooking time (at normal); 15 minutes (at more; 3 minutes (at less). Use this setting with a steamer basket or trivet for best results, so that your food is elevated from the 1 cup of liquid that will also be in the pot.

Slow Cooker: This button will initiate the slow cooker function and set it for a 4-hour cook time. However, you can change the temperature—low will be at 190-201 degrees Fahrenheit; normal is 194-205 degrees Fahrenheit; high is 199-210 degrees Fahrenheit.

Pressure: This button allows you to switch between high and low-pressure settings.

Yogurt: This is an automatic setting that allows you to make yogurt in individual servings. Make sure you find a trustworthy, tested recipe for making yogurt using this function.

Timer: This button allows you to adjust the cooking time by pressing the + or   buttons.

Whole Foods Egg Recipes for Your Instant Pot

Foolproof Hard-Boiled and Soft-Boiled Eggs

Kid-Friendly
20 Minutes or Less
7 Ingredients or Less

Makes 2-12
Prep Time: 1 minute
Cook Time: 3-5 minutes

Ingredients
2-12 eggs (You can cook as many as fit in one layer in the pot.)

Directions
Place the Instant Pot trivet inside the pot. Arrange eggs in one layer on top of the trivet and add 1 cup of water to the pot.

Lock the lid and set the Pressure Release to Sealing. Select the Pressure Cook or Manual setting and set the cooking time to 5 minutes for hard-boiled eggs or 3 minutes for soft-boiled eggs at high pressure.

Once the timer goes off, use a kitchen towel or oven mitts to protect your hand and move the Pressure Release knob to Venting to perform a quick pressure release.

Cool eggs under running water and peel.

Ham and Broccoli Crustless Quiche

Kid-Friendly
7 Ingredients or Less

Serves 2
Prep Time: 10 minutes
Cook Time: 30 minutes

Ingredients
6 eggs
2 teaspoons of ghee, divided
½ cup diced ham
½ cup broccoli florets, chopped small
1 green onion, chopped
¼ teaspoon salt
Pepper to taste

Directions
Place the trivet in the bottom of the Instant Pot and add 1 cup of water to the pot. Grease a 1 quart round oven-safe dish (such as a casserole or soufflé dish) with 1 teaspoon of ghee.

In a medium bowl, beat the eggs and add the remaining 1 teaspoon of ghee and the ham, broccoli, green onion, salt, and pepper. Stir well, then pour into the prepared dish.

Loosely cover the dish with aluminum foil and place inside the Instant Pot on top of the trivet. (Use an aluminum foil sling to lift in and out of the pot, if necessary.)

Lock the lid and set the Pressure Release to Sealing. Select the Pressure Cook or Manual setting and set the cooking time to 30 minutes at high pressure.

Once the timer goes off, let sit for at least 10 minutes; the pressure will release naturally. Then switch the Pressure Release to Venting to allow any last steam out.

Carefully remove the dish from the Instant Pot and serve warm.

Whole Foods Soup Recipes for Your Instant Pot

Creamy Butternut Squash and Sage Soup

Kid-Friendly
7 Ingredients or Less
20 Minutes or Less

Serves 4
Prep Time: 10 minutes
Cook Time: 10 minutes

Ingredients
1 teaspoon olive oil
1 onion, chopped
4 cloves garlic, minced
1 tablespoon fresh sage, or 1 teaspoon ground sage
3 lb. butternut squash, peeled and cut into 1-inch cubes
3 cups chicken broth
½ teaspoon salt
Pepper to taste
½ cup unsweetened coconut milk
Optional: roasted pumpkin seeds for serving

Directions
Select the Sauté setting and heat the olive oil. Add the onion and cook until translucent, about 3-5 minutes. Add the garlic and sage and cook for 1 minute. Add the butternut squash, chicken broth, salt, and pepper, and stir well.

Press Cancel to reset the cooking method. Lock the lid and set the Pressure Release to Sealing. Select the Pressure Cook or Manual setting and set the cooking time to 10 minutes at high pressure.

Once the timer goes off, let sit for at least 10 minutes; the pressure will release naturally. Then switch the Pressure Release to Venting to allow any last steam out.

Open the Instant Pot and puree the soup using an immersion blender or by transferring it to a stand blender. Stir in the unsweetened coconut milk and add salt and pepper to taste.

Notes: For a sweeter soup, add 1 peeled, cored, and diced apple along with the butternut squash.

Luscious and Light Carrot Soup

20 Minutes or Less

Serves 4
Prep Time: 10 minutes
Cook Time: 15 minutes

Ingredients
1 tablespoon ghee
½ yellow onion, chopped
3 cloves garlic, minced
1 tablespoon curry powder
1 teaspoon cayenne pepper (optional)
1½ cups vegetable broth
8-10 large carrots, peeled and chopped
1 14-oz can unsweetened coconut milk

Directions
Select the Sauté setting on the Instant Pot and heat the ghee. Add the onion and garlic and cook, stirring often, until the onion is translucent, 3-5 minutes. Add remaining ingredients, except coconut milk, and stir well.

Press Cancel to reset the cooking method. Lock the lid and set the Pressure Release to Sealing. Select the Pressure Cook or Manual setting and set the cooking time to 15 minutes at high pressure.

Once the timer goes off, let sit for at least 10 minutes; the pressure will release naturally. Then switch the Pressure Release to Venting to allow any last steam out.

Open the Instant Pot and puree the soup using an immersion blender or by transferring it to a stand blender. Stir in the unsweetened coconut milk and add salt and pepper to taste.

My Signature Lemon Chicken Soup

Kid-Friendly

Serves 4
Prep Time: 10 minutes
Cook Time: 6 minutes

Ingredients
2 tablespoons ghee
1 onion, chopped
3 cloves garlic, minced
2 medium carrots, peeled and sliced
3 stalks celery, sliced
8 cups chicken broth
8 oz. mushrooms, sliced
1 tablespoon fresh thyme, or 1 teaspoon dried thyme
Salt to taste
Pepper to taste
1½ lbs. boneless skinless chicken breasts or thighs
1 bunch kale, stemmed and roughly chopped
2 lemons, juiced
Optional: lemon wedges for serving

Directions
Select the Sauté setting and heat the ghee. Add the onion, garlic, carrots, and celery and sauté for 4-6 minutes. Add the chicken broth, mushrooms, and thyme. Taste and add salt and pepper to taste. Add the chicken breasts or thighs and stir well.

Press Cancel to reset the cooking method. Lock the lid and set the Pressure Release to Sealing. Select the Soup setting and set the cooking time to 6 minutes at high pressure.

Once the timer goes off, let sit for at least 10 minutes; the pressure will release naturally. Then switch the Pressure Release to Venting to allow any last steam out.

Open the Instant Pot and remove the chicken and shred. Add the chicken back to the pot and stir in the kale and lemon juice. Ladle into bowls and serve with an extra squeeze of lemon, drizzle of olive oil, or fresh cracked pepper.

Fuss-Free French Onion Soup

7 Ingredients or Less
20 Minutes or Less

Serves 4
Prep Time: 5 minutes
Cook Time: 10 minutes

Ingredients
3 tablespoons ghee
3 large onions, halved and then thinly sliced
1 tablespoon balsamic vinegar
2 tablespoons red wine vinegar
6 cups beef or pork broth
2 large sprigs fresh thyme
1 teaspoon salt

Directions
Select the Sauté setting and heat the ghee. Add the onions and stir constantly until completely cooked down and caramelized. This can take 10-20 minutes or more, depending on your onions and the heat of your Instant Pot. If the onions begin to blacken at the edges, use the Adjust button to reduce the heat to Less.

Once the onions have caramelized, add the balsamic vinegar, red wine vinegar, broth, and thyme, and scrape up any browned bits from the bottom of the pot.

Press Cancel to reset the cooking method. Lock the lid and set the Pressure Release to Sealing. Select the Soup setting and set the cooking time to 10 minutes at high pressure.

Once the timer goes off, let sit for at least 10 minutes; the pressure will release naturally. Then switch the Pressure Release to Venting to allow any last steam out.

Open the Instant Pot and discard the thyme stems. Season with salt and pepper to taste.

Note: Because this soup is so simple, a good quality broth is essential. I recommend Trader Joe's or Pacific's lines broth.

Curried Pumpkin Soup

Kid-Friendly

Serves 4
Prep Time: 10 minutes
Cook Time: 5 minutes

Ingredients
2 tablespoons ghee
1 onion, chopped
2 tablespoons curry powder
1/8 teaspoon cayenne pepper (optional)
4 cups vegetable broth
4 cups pumpkin puree
2 tablespoons coconut aminos
Salt to taste
Pepper to taste
1½ cups unsweetened coconut milk
1 teaspoon lemon juice
Optional: ¼ cup roasted pumpkin seeds for serving

Directions
Select the Sauté setting on the Instant Pot and heat the ghee. Add the onion and cook until translucent, 3-4 minutes.

Add the curry powder and cayenne (if using), and stir until fragrant 1-2 minutes. Add the vegetable broth and 1 cup of water. Stir in the pumpkin puree and coconut aminos. Season to taste with salt and pepper.

Press Cancel to reset the cooking method. Lock the lid and set the Pressure Release to Sealing. Select the Pressure Cook or Manual setting and set the cooking time to 5 minutes at high pressure.

Once the timer goes off, let sit for at least 10 minutes; the pressure will release naturally. Then switch the Pressure Release to Venting to allow any last steam out.

Open the Instant Pot and puree the soup using an immersion blender or by transferring it to a stand blender. Stir in the unsweetened coconut milk and add salt and pepper to taste.

Ladle into bowls and top with roasted pumpkin seeds, if desired.

Creamy Broccoli and Apple Soup

Kid-Friendly
20 Minutes or Less

Serves 4
Prep Time: 5 minutes
Cook Time: 5 minutes

Ingredients
2 tablespoons ghee
3 medium leeks, white parts only (frozen is fine!)
2 shallots, chopped
1 large head broccoli, cut into florets
1 large apple, peeled, cored, and diced
4 cups vegetable broth
1 cup unsweetened coconut milk
Pepper to taste
Salt to taste
Optional: ¼ cup walnuts, toasted
Optional: ¼ cup coconut cream

Directions
Select the Sauté setting and heat the ghee. Add the leeks and shallots and cook, stirring constantly, until softened, 4-6 minutes. Add the broccoli and apple and sauté another 5-6 minutes. Add the vegetable broth and stir well.

Press Cancel to reset the cooking method. Lock the lid and set the Pressure Release to Sealing. Select the Pressure Cook or Manual setting and set the cooking time to 5 minutes at high pressure.

Once the timer goes off, let sit for at least 10 minutes; the pressure will release naturally. Then switch the Pressure Release to Venting to allow any last steam out.

Open the Instant Pot and puree the soup using an immersion blender or by transferring it to a stand blender. Stir in the unsweetened coconut milk and add salt and pepper to taste.

Ladle into bowls and top with toasted walnuts or a drizzle of coconut cream.

Immune-Boost Chard and Sweet Potato Stew

20 Minutes or Less

Serves 2
Prep Time: 10 minutes
Cook Time: 8 minutes

Ingredients
2 tablespoons olive oil
1 teaspoon cumin seeds, or 1 teaspoon ground cumin
1 medium onion, diced
2 medium sweet potatoes, peeled ½ inch cubes
½ teaspoon turmeric
1 tablespoon fresh ginger, peeled and minced
1 teaspoon salt
1 teaspoon ground coriander
2 cups vegetable broth
1 bunch Swiss chard
Optional: lemon wedges for serving

Directions
Select the Sauté setting and heat the olive oil. Add the onion and cook until translucent, 3-5 minutes. If using cumin seeds, add them now and toast them for 1-3 minutes, until fragrant. Otherwise, add the ground cumin in the next step.

Add the sweet potato, ground cumin (if using), ginger, turmeric, coriander, and salt and cook for 3-4 minutes. Add the vegetable broth and chard. Taste and add more salt and pepper if needed.

Press Cancel to reset the cooking method. Lock the lid and set the Pressure Release to Sealing. Select the Pressure Cook or Manual setting and set the cooking time to 8 minutes at high pressure.

Once the timer goes off, let sit for at least 10 minutes; the pressure will release naturally. Then switch the Pressure Release to Venting to allow any last steam out.

Ladle into bowls and serve warm with a squeeze of lemon juice, if desired.

Whole Foods Chicken Recipes for Your Instant Pot

One-Pot Thyme Chicken and Potatoes

Kid-Friendly
20 Minutes or Less

Serves 4
Prep Time: 10 minutes
Cook Time: 10 minutes

Ingredients
2 lbs. boneless skinless chicken breasts
1 teaspoon salt, divided
1 tablespoon olive oil
1 cup chicken broth
2 cloves garlic, minced
1 cup pearl onions (can be frozen), or 1 medium onion, sliced
2 cups carrots, diced
1½ lbs. small potatoes, cut in 1-inch pieces
1 sprig fresh rosemary, or 1 teaspoon dried rosemary
1 sprig fresh thyme, or 1 teaspoon dried thyme
Pepper to taste

Directions
Season the chicken breasts on both sides with ½ teaspoon salt. Select the Sauté setting on the Instant Pot and heat the olive oil. Brown the chicken, about 5 minutes per side.

Add the chicken broth and scraping up any browned bits from the bottom of the pot. Layer in the garlic and onion, top with carrots, and then potatoes. Sprinkle the potatoes with rosemary, thyme, and the remaining ½ teaspoon of salt.

Press Cancel to reset the cooking method. Lock the lid and set the Pressure Release to Sealing. Select the Poultry setting and set the cooking time to 10 minutes.

Once the timer goes off, let sit for at least 10 minutes; the pressure will release naturally. Then switch the Pressure Release to Venting to allow any last steam out.

Open the lid, and add salt and pepper to taste. Serve in bowls with the broth.

Game-Time Buffalo Wings and Cauliflower

Kid-Friendly
20 Minutes or Less
7 Ingredients or Less

Serves 4
Prep Time: 1 minute
Cook Time: 5 minutes

Ingredients
½ cup Frank's Red Hot Sauce
¼ cup ghee
2 lbs. chicken wings
½ head cauliflower, cut into florets

Directions

Add 1 cup of water to the Instant Pot and place the trivet in the pot. Arrange the chicken wings on top of the trivet, then arrange the cauliflower on top of the chicken wings. Be sure you can easily close the lid.

Lock the lid and set the Pressure Release to Sealing. Select the Pressure Cook or Manual setting and set the cooking time to 5 minutes at high pressure.

Meanwhile, in a small bowl, combine the hot sauce and ghee. Set aside.

Once the timer goes off, let sit for 5 minutes, then switch the Pressure Release to Venting to allow any last steam out.

Toss the wings and cauliflower in the buffalo sauce and serve warm.

Optional: For crispier, more charred wings and cauliflower, spread the wings on a baking sheet and the cauliflower on another. Set under the broiler until they reach your desired level of crispiness.

Fiesta Pulled Chicken Taco Bar

Kid-Friendly
7 Ingredients or Less
20 Minutes or Less

Serves 4
Prep Time: 5 minutes
Cook Time: 7-10 minutes

Ingredients
2 pounds of boneless skinless chicken breast or thighs
1 tablespoon chili powder
½ tablespoon ground cumin
½ teaspoon salt
1 cup roasted tomato salsa (Make sure it's corn-free and Whole Foods compliant.)
½ cup chicken broth
1 head butter lettuce
Optional: diced tomatoes, guacamole, green onions, black olives, or any other favorite taco toppings

Directions
Season chicken breasts on both sides with chili powder, cumin, and salt. Place chicken in the pot, pour salsa on top, and toss to coat.

Lock the lid and set the Pressure Release to Sealing. Select the Poultry setting and set the cooking time to 7 minutes for breasts and 10 minutes for thighs at high pressure.

Once the timer goes off, let sit for at least 10 minutes; the pressure will release naturally. Then switch the Pressure Release to Venting to allow any last steam out.

Open the lid and taste, adding more salt and pepper if necessary. Shred the chicken, and allow each person to assemble their own lettuce tacos.

Chicken Marsala with Spaghetti Squash

Kid-Friendly

Serves 5
Prep Time: 10 minutes
Cook Time: 30 minutes

Ingredients
1 large spaghetti squash
2 lbs. boneless skinless chicken breast
1 teaspoon salt
Pepper to taste
1 teaspoon olive oil
2 cloves garlic, minced
1/8 cup champagne vinegar or white wine vinegar
1 cup sliced mushrooms
½ cup chicken broth
Optional: 1 teaspoon arrowroot powder
Optional: fresh basil for serving

Directions
Place the trivet inside the Instant Pot, add 1 cup water, and place the spaghetti squash on the trivet. Lock the lid and set the Pressure Release to Sealing. Select the Manual or Pressure Cook setting and set the timer to 20 minutes at high pressure. Once the timer goes off, let sit for at least 10 minutes; the pressure will release naturally. Then switch the Pressure Release to Venting to allow any last steam out. Remove the spaghetti squash and set aside to cool.

Discard the water, dry the pot, and select the Sauté setting. Heat the olive oil, then add the chicken, salt, and pepper to taste. Sear the chicken until browned, about 5 minutes on each side. Add the garlic, vinegar, mushrooms, and broth, and stir to combine, scraping up any browned bits from the bottom of the pan.

Lock the lid and set the Pressure Release to Sealing. Select the Poultry setting and set the cooking time to 7 minutes at high pressure.

Meanwhile, slice the spaghetti squash in half, scoop out the seeds, and separate the squash from the rind. Once the Instant Pot timer goes off, use a kitchen towel or oven mitts to protect your hand and move the Pressure Release knob to Venting to perform a quick pressure release.

Open the lid and taste, adding more salt and pepper if necessary. Serve the chicken over the spaghetti squash noodles and top with the marsala sauce, mushrooms, and fresh basil, if desired

Note: For a thicker sauce, remove ¼ cup of the marsala sauce. Dissolve 1 teaspoon arrowroot powder in the sauce, then add back to the pot and mix well. Allow to cook for a few minutes, until thickened.

Lemon Pepper Chicken with Baby Potatoes

Kid-Friendly
7 Ingredients or Less

Serves 4
Prep Time: 15 minutes
Cook Time: 15 minutes

Ingredients
3 lemons, zested and juiced
1 teaspoon garlic powder
1½ teaspoons black pepper
1 teaspoon salt
1 tablespoon ghee
2 lbs. bone-in chicken thighs
1 cup chicken broth
1 lb. baby potatoes, or 1 lb. large potatoes cut into 1-inch pieces

Directions

In a small bowl, combine the lemon zest, garlic powder, pepper, and salt.

Select the Sauté setting and heat the ghee. Season the chicken thighs on both sides with the lemon pepper rub. Add the chicken thighs to the pot and brown well on each side, about 4 minutes per side. You may need to work in batches.

Add chicken broth and scrape up any browned bits from the bottom of the pot. Add the potatoes and season lightly with more salt and pepper.

Lock the lid and set the Pressure Release to Sealing. Select the Poultry setting and set the cooking time to 15 minutes at high pressure.

Once the timer goes off, use a kitchen towel or oven mitts to protect your hand and move the Pressure Release knob to Venting to perform a quick pressure release.

Open the lid, and taste, adding more salt and pepper if necessary. Drizzle with the lemon juice, and if desired, olive oil, before serving.

Cranberry and Balsamic Chicken

20 Minutes or Less

Serves 4
Prep Time: 5 minutes
Cook Time: 10 minutes

Ingredients
2 lbs. boneless skinless chicken thighs
1 tablespoon olive oil
½ teaspoon salt
Pepper to taste
½ small red onion, diced
1 cup cranberry juice (Be sure it is no sugar added.)
3 tablespoons balsamic vinegar
1 tablespoon coconut aminos
½ tablespoon garlic powder
½ tablespoon dried rosemary
Optional: almond flour

Directions
Select the Sauté setting and heat the olive oil. Season the thighs with salt and pepper, then brown on one side, 4-5 minutes. Flip the thighs, add the red onion, and allow both to brown for 4-5 minutes more.

Meanwhile, in a small bowl, mix the cranberry juice, balsamic vinegar, coconut aminos, garlic powder, and dried rosemary. Add to the Instant Pot and stir, scraping up any browned bits from the bottom of the pot.

Lock the lid and set the Pressure Release to Sealing. Select the Poultry setting and set the cooking time to 10 minutes at high pressure.

With a kitchen towel or oven mitts protecting your hand, move the Pressure Release knob to Venting to perform a quick pressure release. Open the lid and taste, adding more salt and pepper if necessary. Remove the chicken, transfer to a platter, and serve with the sauce.

Note: For a thicker sauce, remove ¼ cup of the sauce. Dissolve 1 teaspoon arrowroot powder in the sauce, then add back to the pot and mix well. Allow to cook for a few minutes, until thickened.

The Easiest Indian Chicken Curry

20 Minutes or Less

Serves 4
Prep Time: 10 minutes
Cook Time: 8 minutes

Ingredients
1 tablespoon ghee
1½ large yellow onion, chopped
1 teaspoon salt
2 teaspoons garlic powder
2 teaspoons ground ginger
2 heaping teaspoons turmeric
¼ teaspoon cayenne powder
2 teaspoons paprika
2 teaspoons garam masala
1-16-oz can stewed tomatoes, partially drained
1/2 cup tomato paste
2-14 oz. cans unsweetened coconut milk
2 lbs. boneless skinless chicken breasts or thighs

Directions
Select the Sauté setting and heat the ghee. Add the onion and cook until translucent, about 3-5 minutes. Add the salt, garlic powder, ground ginger, turmeric, cayenne, paprika, and garam masala, and sauté for 2 minutes. Add the canned tomatoes, tomato paste, and unsweetened coconut milk and mix well. Add the chicken breasts or thighs and stir to coat in the sauce.

Lock the lid and set the Pressure Release to Sealing. Select the Poultry setting and set the cooking time to 8 minutes at high pressure.

Once the timer goes off, let sit for at least 10 minutes; the pressure will release naturally. Then switch the Pressure Release to Venting to allow any last steam out.

Open the lid and taste, adding more salt and pepper if necessary. Break the chicken into smaller pieces but don't fully shred it. Serve with zoodles or cucumber noodles.

Better-Than-the-Store Rotisserie Chicken

Kid-Friendly
7 Ingredients or Less

Serves 6
Prep Time: 15 minutes
Cook Time: 20 minutes

Ingredients
1 4-5 pound whole chicken
1 ½ teaspoons salt
Pepper to taste
2 teaspoons garlic powder
2 tablespoons olive oil
1 teaspoon thyme
1 lemon, juiced and zested
1 cup chicken broth

Directions
Pat the chicken dry with paper towels. In a small bowl, mix salt, pepper, garlic powder, olive oil, thyme, and lemon juice and zest. Rub the chicken with the herb oil.

Select the Sauté setting and add the chicken, back side down, to the pot. Sear for 6-7 minutes, until well browned, then flip and brown the breast side for another 6-7 minutes. Add the chicken broth and scrape up any browned bits stuck to the bottom of the pot.

Lock the lid and set the Pressure Release to Sealing. Select the Poultry setting and set the cooking time to 20 minutes at high pressure.

Once the timer goes off, use a kitchen towel or oven mitts to protect your hand and move the Pressure Release knob to Venting to perform a quick pressure release.

Open the lid, and taste, adding more salt and pepper to the sauce if necessary. Transfer to a platter, carve, and serve warm.

Our Go-To BBQ Drumsticks

Kid-Friendly
20 Minutes or Less
7 Ingredients or Less

Serves 4
Prep Time: 10 minutes
Cook Time: 20 minutes

Ingredients
½ cup unsweetened apple juice
¼ cup tomato paste
1 teaspoon garlic powder
1 teaspoon onion powder
1 teaspoon paprika
¼ teaspoon cayenne pepper (Or ½ teaspoon, if you like spicy BBQ sauce.)
½ teaspoon salt
2 tablespoons apple cider vinegar
Optional: 1 teaspoon liquid smoke
4-12 chicken drumsticks

Directions
Select the Sauté setting on the Instant Pot. Add all of the ingredients except the drumsticks and stir well. Allow to cook for at least 10 minutes, until thickened. Taste and adjust salt or spice level to your taste.

Ladle the sauce out of the Instant Pot, but no need to wipe it clean. Add 1 cup of water to the pot and place the trivet in the bottom of the pot. Arrange the drumsticks on top of the trivet.

Lock the lid and set the Pressure Release to Sealing. Select the Poultry setting and set the cooking time to 20 minutes at high pressure.

Once the timer goes off, let sit for at least 10 minutes, then switch the Pressure Release to Venting to allow any last steam out. Toss the drumsticks in the BBQ sauce and serve warm.

Optional: For crispier, more charred drumsticks, spread the drumsticks on a baking sheet and set under the broiler until they reach your desired level of char.

Note: This barbeque sauce will be less sweet than you might be used to, because it has no added sugar. To add more sweetness, you can puree 5 pitted dates in a food processor with a bit of water and incorporate into the sauce. Or, if you're in a pinch, you can always use a high-quality Whole Foods compliant sauce.

Whole Foods Seafood Recipes for Your Instant Pot

Takeout Asian Salmon & Broccoli

Kid-Friendly
20 Minutes or Less

Serves 4
Prep Time: 5 minutes
Cook Time: 3 minutes

Ingredients:
2 cloves garlic, minced
¼ teaspoon crushed red pepper
½ teaspoon salt
Pepper to taste
3 tablespoons coconut aminos
1 cup chicken broth
2 cups broccoli florets
4 medium-sized salmon fillets
½ lime, juiced
1 tablespoon sesame oil

Directions
In a small bowl, combine half of the minced garlic, crushed red pepper, salt, pepper, and 2 tablespoons of the coconut aminos. Brush the sauce on the salmon fillets.

In the Instant Pot, add 1 cup of chicken broth and place the trivet in the bottom of the pot. Add the broccoli florets, and season to taste with salt and pepper. Arrange the salmon fillets on top of the broccoli.

Lock the lid and set the Pressure Release to Sealing. Select the Steam setting and set the cooking time to 3 minutes at high pressure. Meanwhile, in a small bowl, combine the lime juice, remaining minced garlic, remaining 1 tablespoon of coconut aminos, sesame oil, and salt and pepper to taste.

With a kitchen towel or oven mitts protecting your hand, move the Pressure Release knob to Venting to perform a quick pressure release.

Open the lid and taste, adding more salt and pepper if necessary. Serve the salmon and broccoli with the sesame oil sauce.

Easy Lemon Garlic Salmon with Green Beans

Kid-Friendly
20 Minutes or Less
7 Ingredients or Less

Serves 4
Prep Time: 5 minutes
Cook Time: 3 minutes

Ingredients:
4 cloves garlic, minced
1 teaspoon salt, divided
Pepper to taste
2 tablespoons ghee, divided
2 tablespoons lemon juice, divided
1 medium onion, sliced
3 cups green beans, trimmed
4 medium-sized salmon fillets

Directions

In a small bowl, combine half of the minced garlic, ½ teaspoon salt, pepper, and 1 tablespoon each of the ghee and lemon juice. Brush the lemon garlic sauce on the salmon fillets.

In the Instant Pot, add 1 cup of chicken broth and place the trivet in the bottom of the pot. Add the onions and green beans, and season lightly with salt and pepper. Arrange the salmon fillets on top of the onions and green beans.

Lock the lid and set the Pressure Release to Sealing. Select the Steam setting and set the cooking time to 3 minutes at high pressure. Meanwhile, in a small bowl, combine the remaining minced garlic, remaining 1 tablespoon of ghee, lemon juice, and salt and pepper to taste.

With a kitchen towel or oven mitts protecting your hand, move the Pressure Release knob to Venting to perform a quick pressure release.

Open the lid and taste, adding more salt and pepper if necessary. Serve the salmon and green beans with the lemon garlic sauce.

Light and Fresh Mediterranean Cod

20 Minutes or Less

Serves 4
Prep Time: 10 minutes
Cook Time: 6 minutes

Ingredients
1 tablespoon ghee
1 lemon, juiced
1 onion, sliced
½ teaspoon salt
½ teaspoon black pepper
1 teaspoon dried oregano
1-28 oz. can diced tomatoes
2 tablespoons capers, drained, or 2 tablespoons Kalamata olives, chopped
6 cod fillets

Directions
Select the Sauté setting and heat the ghee. Add the remaining ingredients, except for the cod. Cook the sauce for 10 minutes. Place the cod fillets in the sauce and spoon sauce over each fillet.

Lock the lid and set the Pressure Release to Sealing. Select the Steam setting and set the cooking time to 3 minutes at high pressure.

Once the timer has gone off and with a kitchen towel or oven mitts protecting your hand, move the Pressure Release knob to Venting to perform a quick pressure release.

Open the lid and taste the sauce, adding more salt and pepper if necessary. Serve the cod with the Mediterranean tomato sauce.

5-Minute Citrus Shrimp

Kid-Friendly
20 Minutes or Less
7 Ingredients or Less

Serves 4
Prep Time: 5 minutes
Cook Time: 1 minute

Ingredients
1 tablespoon ghee
4 garlic cloves, minced
½ cup orange juice (100% pure, no sugar added)
½ cup chicken broth
2 pounds of peeled and deveined raw shrimp
2 tablespoons lemon juice
½ teaspoon salt
Pepper to taste

Directions
Select the Sauté setting and heat the ghee. Add the garlic and cook until fragrant, 1-2 minutes. Add the orange juice and chicken broth.

Press Cancel to reset the cooking method, add the shrimp, and season with ½ teaspoon salt. Lock the lid and set the Pressure Release to Sealing. Select the Steam setting and set the cooking time to 1 minute at high pressure.

Once the timer has gone off and with a kitchen towel or oven mitts protecting your hand, move the Pressure Release knob to Venting to perform a quick pressure release.

Open the lid and stir in lemon juice and adjust salt and pepper to taste. Serve over cauliflower rice or mixed vegetables.

Whole Foods Pork Recipes for Your Instant Pot

Sunday Favorite Pork Ragu

Kid-Friendly
7 Ingredients or Less

Serves 4
Prep Time: 5 minutes
Cook Time: 45 minutes

Ingredients
18 oz. pork tenderloin
1 teaspoon salt
Pepper to taste
1 tablespoon olive oil
6 garlic cloves
1-28 oz. can crushed tomatoes
2 sprigs of fresh thyme, or 2 teaspoons dried thyme
1 teaspoon dried oregano
Optional: 2 bay leaves

Directions
Season the pork loin with salt and pepper. Select the Sauté setting on the Instant Pot and heat the olive oil. Add the pork loin to the Instant Pot and sear on all sides until browned. Add the garlic, crushed tomatoes, thyme, oregano, and if using, bay leaves.

Lock the lid and set the Pressure Release to Sealing. Select the Meat/Stew setting and set the cooking time to 45 minutes at high pressure.

Once the timer goes off, let sit for at least 10 minutes; the pressure will release naturally. Then switch the Pressure Release to Venting to allow any last steam out.

Open the lid and taste, adding more salt and pepper if necessary. Shred the pork and serve over spaghetti squash or spoon over vegetable fritters.

Pear Smothered Pork Chops

7 Ingredients or Less
20 Minutes or Less

Serves 4
Prep Time: 10 minutes
Cook Time: 3 minutes

Ingredients
4-½ inch thick bone-in pork chops
1 teaspoon salt
½ teaspoon ground black pepper
1 tablespoon ghee
2 medium yellow onions, cut into 8 wedges
2 large Bosc pears, peeled, cored, and cut into 4 wedges
½ cup unsweetened pear juice
¼ cup chicken broth
½ teaspoon ground allspice

Directions
Season the pork chops with salt and pepper. Select the Sauté setting on the Instant Pot and heat the ghee. Brown the chops on both sides then remove to a plate, working in batches of 2 chops at a time if necessary.

Add the onion and pears and cook for 3 minutes until pears are lightly browned. Add the pear juice, chicken broth, and allspice and stir. Nestle the pork chops back into the sauce.

Lock the lid and set the Pressure Release to Sealing. Select the Meat/Stew setting and set the cooking time to 3 minutes at high pressure.

Once the timer has gone off and with a kitchen towel or oven mitts protecting your hand, move the Pressure Release knob to Venting to perform a quick pressure release.

Open the lid and taste, adding more salt and pepper if necessary. Remove the pork chops to a platter and serve smothered in the pear sauce.

Artichoke and Lemon Pork Chops

Kid-Friendly

Serves 4
Prep Time: 10 minutes
Cook Time: 3 minutes

Ingredients
3 oz. bacon, diced
4-½ inch thick bone-in pork chops
2 teaspoons ground black pepper
1 shallot, minced
1 teaspoon lemon zest
3 garlic cloves, minced
1 teaspoon dried rosemary
1 cup chicken broth
1 9-oz package frozen artichoke heart quarters

Directions
Select the Sauté setting and add the bacon. Cook until it has rendered its fat and turned crispy, about 5 minutes. Transfer the bacon to a plate.

Season the pork chops with salt and pepper and add to the Instant Pot. Brown the chops on both sides then remove to a plate, working in batches of 2 chops at a time if necessary.

Add shallots to the pot and cook for 1 minute. Add lemon zest, garlic, and rosemary and cook until fragrant. Add the chicken broth, artichokes, and cooked bacon. Stir well then nestle the chops back into the sauce.

Press Cancel to reset the cooking method. Lock the lid and set the Pressure Release to Sealing. Select the Meat/Stew setting and set the cooking time to 3 minutes at high pressure.

Once the timer has gone off and with a kitchen towel or oven mitts protecting your hand, move the Pressure Release knob to Venting to perform a quick pressure release.

Open the lid and taste, adding salt and pepper if necessary. Serve the pork chops with the lemon artichoke sauce.

Cuban Pulled Pork

Kid-Friendly
7 Ingredients or Less

Serve: 8
Prep Time: 5 minutes
Cook Time: 80 minutes

Ingredients
3 lbs. boneless pork shoulder, fat trimmed
6 cloves garlic
2/3 cup grapefruit juice (100% juice, no sugar added)
½ tablespoon fresh oregano, or 1 teaspoon dried oregano
½ tablespoon cumin
1 lime, juiced
½ tablespoon salt
1 bay leaf
Optional for serving: lime wedges, cilantro, salsa, or hot sauce

Directions
Cut the pork shoulder into 4 evenly sized pieces. In a blender or food processor, combine the garlic, grapefruit juice, oregano, cumin, lime juice, and salt, and blend until combined. Place the pork shoulder pieces in the Instant Pot and rub with the sauce.

Lock the lid and set the Pressure Release to Sealing. Select the Meat/Stew setting and set the cooking time to 80 minutes at high pressure.

Once the timer goes off, let sit for at least 10 minutes; the pressure will release naturally. Then switch the Pressure Release to Venting to allow any last steam out.

Open the lid and taste, adding more salt and pepper if necessary. Remove the pork, shred, ladle sauce over it, and serve warm.

Note: For a thicker sauce, add the shredded pork back to the Instant Pot with the sauce. Select the Sauté setting and cook for 3-5 minutes until sauce has soaked into the pork.

5-Ingredient Kahlua Pork

Kid-Friendly
7 Ingredients or Less

Serves 8
Prep Time: 15 minutes
Cook Time: 80 minutes

Ingredients
3 lbs. boneless pork shoulder, fat trimmed
5 bacon slices
1 teaspoon salt
Pepper to taste
1 cup chicken or pork broth
6 cloves garlic
½ cup diced pineapple, fresh or canned
1 tablespoon liquid smoke

Directions
Select the Sauté setting and add the bacon. Cook until the bacon has rendered its fat and turned crispy, about 5 minutes. Transfer the bacon to a plate.

Cut the pork shoulder into 4 evenly sized pieces and season with salt and pepper. Add to the Instant Pot and sear on all sides until brown, about 4-6 minutes per side. Add 1 cup of chicken or pork broth, pineapple, garlic, and liquid smoke.

Lock the lid and set the Pressure Release to Sealing. Select the Meat/Stew setting and set the cooking time to 80 minutes at high pressure.

Once the timer goes off, let sit for at least 10 minutes; the pressure will release naturally. Then switch the Pressure Release to Venting to allow any last steam out.

Open the lid and taste, adding more salt and pepper if necessary. Remove the pork, shred it, ladle sauce over it, and serve warm.

Note: For a thicker sauce, add the shredded pork back to the Instant Pot with the sauce. Select the Sauté setting and cook for 3-5 minutes until sauce has soaked into the pork.

Apple and Herb Pork Tenderloin

Kid-Friendly
7 Ingredients or Less

Serves 4
Prep Time: 15 minutes
Cook Time: 12 minutes

Ingredients
2 tablespoons ghee
1 teaspoon of salt
½ teaspoon black pepper
1 lb. boneless pork tenderloin
1 large red onion, thinly sliced
2 medium green apples, peeled, cored, and diced
4 fresh thyme sprigs, or 1 tablespoon dried thyme
1 cup of chicken broth

Optional: use ½ cup chicken broth and ½ cup apple cider)

Directions
Select the Sauté setting and heat the ghee. Season the pork loin on all sides with salt and pepper. Add to the Instant Pot and sear on all sides until brown, about 3-4 minutes per side. Transfer the loin to a plate and set aside.

Add red onion to the Instant Pot and cook for 3-5 minutes, until translucent. Add apples, thyme, and chicken broth, stir well, then nestle the pork loin back into the Instant Pot.

Lock the lid and set the Pressure Release to Sealing. Select the Meat/Stew setting and set the cooking time to 15 minutes at high pressure.

Once the timer goes off, let sit for at least 10 minutes; the pressure will release naturally. Then switch the Pressure Release to Venting to allow any last steam out.

Open the lid and taste, adding more salt and pepper if necessary. Transfer the pork loin to a cutting board and allow to rest for 5 minutes. Slice and serve with the apple and herb sauce.

Cumin-Spiced Pulled Pork Carnitas

Kid-Friendly

Serves 6
Prep Time: 7 minutes
Cook Time: 40 minutes

Ingredients
3 lb. boneless pork shoulder, fat trimmed
2 tablespoons of olive oil
¾ cup chicken or pork broth
1 head butter lettuce
2 carrots, grated
2 limes, cut into wedges

For spice rub:
1 tablespoon cumin
1 tablespoon garlic powder
½ tablespoon salt
2 teaspoons oregano
1 teaspoon pepper
1 teaspoon coriander
½ teaspoon cayenne pepper

Directions
In a large bowl, combine the ingredients for the spice rub. Quarter the pork shoulder in 4 evenly sized pieces and rub all over with the cumin spice rub. Allow the pork to absorb the spice rub for 30 minutes or up to overnight in the refrigerator.

Select the Sauté setting and heat the olive oil. Add the pork shoulder to the Instant Pot and sear on all sides until brown, about 3-4 minutes per side. Add ¾ cup of chicken or pork broth and scrape up any browned bits at the bottom of the pot.

Lock the lid and set the Pressure Release to Sealing. Select the Meat/Stew setting and set the cooking time to 40 minutes at high pressure.

Once the timer goes off, let sit for at least 10 minutes; the pressure will release naturally. Then switch the Pressure Release to Venting to allow any last steam out.

Remove the lid and taste the sauce; adjust seasoning if necessary. Shred the pork shoulder and serve in butter lettuce cups, topped with grated carrot and a squeeze of lime.

Optional: For a thicker sauce, add the shredded pork back to the Instant Pot with the sauce. Select the Sauté setting and cook for 3-5 minutes until sauce has soaked into the pork.

Whole Foods Beef Recipes for Your Instant Pot

Steak Fajita Stuffed Baked Potatoes

Kid-Friendly

Prep Time: 15 Minutes
Cook Time: 20 minutes

2 tablespoons olive oil, divided
1 ½ lbs. skirt steak, sliced
2 green bell peppers, seeded and sliced
1 red bell pepper, seeded and sliced
1 onion, sliced
¾ cup beef broth
4 medium potatoes
Optional: lime wedges for serving

For fajita seasoning:
1 tablespoon cumin
½ tablespoon chili powder
2 teaspoons garlic powder
¼ teaspoon cayenne pepper, or to taste
1 teaspoon dried oregano
1 teaspoon salt
½ teaspoon black pepper

In a small bowl, combine the chili powder, cumin, garlic powder, cayenne pepper, oregano, salt, and pepper. Pick the potatoes all over with a fork to allow steam to vent and wrap them in aluminum foil.

Select the Sauté setting on the Instant Pot and heat 1 tablespoon of the olive oil. Add half of the steak and sear on all sides. Remove to a plate and sear the second half of the steak. Remove to a plate again. Add the remaining 1 tablespoon of olive oil to the Instant Pot, then add the onion and bell peppers. Sauté until cooked down and seared.

Add the beef broth to the Instant Pot and scrape up any browned bits from the bottom of the pot. Add the steak and spice mix and stir well. Place the trivet over the steak and vegetables. Place the foil-wrapped potatoes on top of the trivet. (It's okay if they get a bit wet with sauce.)

Press Cancel to reset the cooking method. Lock the lid and set the Pressure Release to Sealing. Select the Meat/Stew setting and set the cooking time to 20 minutes at high pressure.

Once the timer goes off, let sit for at least 10 minutes; the pressure will release naturally. Then switch the Pressure Release to Venting to allow any last steam out.

Remove the baked potatoes, slice open, and stuff with the steak and vegetable fajitas. Serve with a squeeze of lime or guacamole.

Guilt-Free Beef Goulash

Kid-Friendly

Serves 6
Prep Time: 15 minutes
Cook Time: 15 minutes

Ingredients
2 lbs. extra lean ground beef
2 tablespoons olive oil, divided
1 teaspoon salt
½ teaspoon pepper
1 large onion, sliced
1 large red bell pepper, stemmed, seeded, and sliced
4 cloves garlic, minced
2 tablespoons sweet paprika
½ teaspoon cayenne pepper (or less, if you don't like spicy food)
4 cups beef broth
2-15 oz. cans diced tomatoes

Directions
Select the Sauté setting and heat 1 tablespoon of the olive oil. Add the ground beef and cook, stirring to break up large chunks. Season with salt and pepper, and sear until ground beef is very well-browned. Transfer to a bowl.

Heat remaining tablespoon of olive oil in the Instant Pot, and add onion and bell pepper. Cook, stirring occasionally, until beginning to brown, 6-8 minutes. Add garlic, paprika, cayenne pepper and cook for 2-3 minutes, stirring constantly. Add beef broth, diced tomatoes, and cooked ground beef and stir well.

Press Cancel to reset the cooking method. Lock the lid and set the Pressure Release to Sealing. Select the Soup setting and set the cooking time to 15 minutes at low pressure.

When the timer goes off, use a kitchen towel or oven mitts to protect your hand and move the Pressure Release knob to Venting to perform a quick pressure release.

Open the lid and taste, adding more salt and pepper if necessary. Serve goulash spooned over spaghetti squash or carrot noodles.

Rosemary Braised Beef Short Ribs

7 Ingredients or Less

Serves 5
Prep Time: 10 minutes
Cook Time: 45 minutes

Ingredients
4 pounds beef short ribs
½ tablespoon salt
1 tablespoon olive oil
1 medium onion, quartered
6 cloves garlic, minced
¼ cup red wine vinegar
1½ cup beef broth
1 tablespoon fresh rosemary, or 1 ½ teaspoons dried rosemary

Directions
Season short ribs all over with salt. Select the Sauté setting on the Instant Pot and heat the olive oil. Brown the ribs on all sides, working in batches if necessary.

Add onion, garlic, red wine vinegar, beef broth, and rosemary to the Instant Pot, turning the ribs to coat them well.

Press Cancel to reset the cooking method. Lock the lid and set the Pressure Release to Sealing. Select the Meat/Stew setting and set the cooking time to 45 minutes at high pressure.

Once the timer goes off, let sit for at least 10 minutes; the pressure will release naturally. Then switch the Pressure Release to Venting to allow any last steam out.

Open the pot and taste the sauce; adjust the seasoning if necessary. Spoon the ribs and sauce over cauliflower rice or roasted brussels sprouts.

One-Pot Beef, Potato, and Zucchini Stew

Kid-Friendly

Serves 6
Prep Time: 10 minutes
Cook Time: 35 minutes

Ingredients
1 lb. beef stew meat, cubed
1 teaspoon salt
½ teaspoon pepper
1 tablespoon olive oil
1 medium onion, chopped
1 medium zucchini, sliced
1 ½ lbs. small waxy potatoes, in 2-inch pieces
4 medium carrots, sliced
2 cups beef broth
1 tablespoon red wine vinegar
1 teaspoon paprika
1 teaspoon onion powder
1 tablespoon tomato paste
Optional: 1 teaspoon arrowroot powder

Directions
Season the meat with salt and pepper. Select the Sauté setting on the Instant Pot and heat the olive oil. Sear the meat until well-browned, 8-10 minutes. Add the onion, zucchini, potatoes, carrots, beef broth, red wine vinegar, paprika, onion powder, and tomato paste and stir well.

Press Cancel to reset the cooking method. Lock the lid and set the Pressure Release to Sealing. Select the Meat/Stew setting and set the cooking time to 35 minutes at high pressure.

Once the timer goes off, let sit for at least 10 minutes; the pressure will release naturally. Then switch the Pressure Release to Venting to allow any last steam out.

Open the pot and taste the stew; adjust the seasoning if necessary.

Optional: For a thicker stew, ladle ¼ cup of the sauce into a small bowl and mix in 1 teaspoon arrowroot powder. Pour back into the Instant Pot, stir, and cook on the Sauté setting until thickened.

Simplest Beef Stroganoff

Kid-Friendly
20 Minutes or Less

Serves 4
Prep Time: 10 minutes
Cook Time: 18 minutes

Ingredients
1 tablespoon almond flour
1 teaspoon salt
¼ teaspoon pepper
1 lb. beef stew meat, cut into strips
1 tablespoon olive oil
1 onion, chopped
3 cloves garlic, minced
1 cup mushrooms, sliced
2 tablespoons tomato paste
3 tablespoons red wine vinegar
2 cups beef broth

Directions
In a large bowl, mix the almond flour, salt, and pepper. Add the beef strips and toss to coat well. Select the Sauté setting on the Instant Pot and heat the olive oil. Shake any excess flour from the beef and sauté until well-browned. Add the remaining ingredients to the Instant Pot.

Press Cancel to reset the cooking method. Lock the lid and set the Pressure Release to Sealing. Select the Meat/Stew setting and set the cooking time to 18 minutes at medium pressure.

Once the timer goes off, let sit for at least 10 minutes; the pressure will release naturally. Then switch the Pressure Release to Venting to allow any last steam out.

Open the lid and taste, adding more salt and pepper if necessary. Serve with zucchini noodles or roasted potatoes.

Mexican Meatloaf with Baby Potatoes

Kid-Friendly

Serves 4
Prep Time: 10 minutes
Cook Time: 20 minutes

1 cup beef broth
1 tablespoon ghee
1 teaspoon salt
½ teaspoon black pepper
1 ½ lbs. large baby potatoes, about 1 inch each
1 pound ground beef
1 cup roasted salsa, plus extra for serving (Make sure it's corn-free and Whole Foods compliant.)
1 onion, finely chopped
1 egg

Five spice mix:
1 tablespoon cumin
½ tablespoon chili powder
1 teaspoon garlic powder
1 teaspoon oregano
1 teaspoon onion powder
1 teaspoon salt
¼ teaspoon black pepper

In the bottom of the Instant Pot, stir the beef broth, ghee, salt, and pepper. Add the potatoes and toss to coat. Place the Instant Pot trivet on top of the potatoes.

In a large bowl, combine the Five Spice mix. Add the ground beef, roasted salsa, onion, and egg, and mix until well incorporated. Set the meatloaf mix on a large piece of heavy duty foil or two sheets of regular strength foil. Shape the meat into a loaf, the wrap the foil around it like a boat, leaving the top open. Gently place the foil-wrapped meatloaf on top of the trivet inside the Instant Pot.

Lock the lid and set the Pressure Release to Sealing. Select the Meat/Stew setting and set the cooking time to 20 minutes at high pressure.

Once the timer goes off, use a kitchen towel or oven mitts to protect your hand and move the Pressure Release knob to Venting to perform a quick pressure release.

Open the lid and taste, adding more salt and pepper if necessary. Brush the meatloaf with more salsa if desired, and serve alongside the potatoes and your favorite Mexican toppings.

Note: For picky eaters, use less of the Five Spice mix for a subtler flavor.

Lone Star State Beef Chili

Kid-Friendly

Serves 4
Prep Time: 10 minutes
Cook Time: 35 minutes

Ingredients
1 lb. ground beef
1 green bell pepper, seeded and diced
1 large onion, chopped
1 medium carrot, finely diced
¼ teaspoon black pepper
1 teaspoon salt
1 teaspoon onion powder
1 tablespoon lime juice
1 tablespoon chili powder
1 teaspoon paprika
2 teaspoons garlic powder
2 teaspoons cumin
2-14 oz. cans fire roasted tomatoes

Directions
Select the Sauté setting, add the ground beef, and cook until browned. (For more flavor, cook the beef past browned, until it begins to sear a bit and get darker.) Add all remaining ingredients and stir well, scraping up any browned bits from the bottom of the pot.

Press Cancel to reset the cooking method. Lock the lid and set the Pressure Release to Sealing. Select the Meat/Stew setting and set the cooking time to 35 minutes at high pressure.

Once the timer goes off, use a kitchen towel or oven mitts to protect your hand and move the Pressure Release knob to Venting to perform a quick pressure release.

Open the lid and taste, adding salt, pepper, or hot sauce, if necessary. Serve over cauliflower steaks or baked potatoes, or ladle into a bowl and top with guacamole.

Skinny Sloppy Joes

Kid-Friendly
20 Minutes or Less

Serves 4
Prep Time: 10 minutes
Cook Time: 10 minutes

Ingredients
1 tablespoon ghee
1 lb. ground beef
1 teaspoon salt
¼ teaspoon pepper
1 bell pepper, finely chopped
1 onion, finely chopped
3 cloves garlic, minced
1 14-oz can tomato sauce
1 tablespoon apple cider vinegar
1 tablespoon Dijon mustard

Directions
Select the Sauté setting on the Instant Pot and heat 1 tablespoon of ghee. Add the ground beef, salt, and pepper and brown well. (For more flavor, cook the beef past browned, until it begins to sear a bit and get darker.)

Add the bell pepper, onion, and garlic and cook 4-6 minutes, until softened. Add the tomato sauce, vinegar, and mustard.

Press Cancel to reset the cooking method. Lock the lid and set the Pressure Release to Sealing. Select the Meat/Stew setting and set the cooking time to 10 minutes at high pressure.

Once the timer goes off, use a kitchen towel or oven mitts to protect your hand and move the Pressure Release knob to Venting to perform a quick pressure release.

Open the pot and taste the stew; adjust the seasoning if necessary. Serve over cauliflower steaks or as the filling to a baked potato.

Note: These Sloppy Joes will be less sweet than you might be used to, because they don't rely on sugar-packed ketchup. To add more sweetness, you can puree 5 pitted dates in a food processor with a bit of water and incorporate into the sauce before pressure cooking.

Whole Foods Vegetable Recipes for Your Instant Pot

Perfect Potato and Cauliflower Mash

Kid-Friendly
7 Ingredients or Less
20 Minutes or Less

Serves 4
Prep Time: 5 minutes
Cook Time: 8 minutes

Ingredients
2 lbs. russet potatoes, peeled and diced into 1-inch pieces
8 oz. cauliflower florets (approximately 1 head)
4 cups chicken broth
½ teaspoon salt
4 tablespoons ghee
½ tablespoon garlic powder

Directions
Add the cauliflower and potatoes to the Instant Pot and cover with the chicken broth. Lock the lid and set the Pressure Release to Sealing. Select the Pressure Cook or Manual setting and set the cooking time to 8 minutes at high pressure.

Once the timer goes off, use a kitchen towel or oven mitts to protect your hand and move the Pressure Release knob to Venting to perform a quick pressure release.

Drain, reserving any excess broth, and return the potatoes and cauliflower to the pot. With a potato masher, immersion blender, or fork, mash to your desired consistency, adding broth as needed for more moisture. Stir in the ghee and garlic powder, and add salt and pepper to taste.

Note: For more flavor, mix in fresh herbs such as thyme or rosemary before serving. You can also stir in ½ cup unsweetened original almond milk for a creamier mash, or use only cauliflower for a lighter mash.

Sage and Garlic Spaghetti Squash

20 Minutes or Less
7 Ingredients or Less

Serves 4
Prep Time: 5 minutes
Cook Time: 15 minutes

Ingredients
1 medium spaghetti squash
2 tablespoons olive oil
5 garlic cloves, minced
1 tablespoons fresh sage, chopped
1 teaspoon salt
1/8 teaspoon nutmeg
Pepper to taste

Directions
Halve the squash and scoop out any seeds. In the Instant Pot, add 1 cup of water and place the trivet inside. Arrange the two squash halves on the trivet so that the flesh side is facing up. This can either be done side-by-side or stacked on top of each other, depending on the size of your squash and your Instant Pot.

Lock the lid and set the Pressure Release to Sealing. Select the Pressure Cook or Manual setting and set the cooking time to 7 minutes at high pressure.

As the squash pressure cooks, heat the olive oil in a small skillet. Add the garlic, sage, salt, nutmeg, and pepper to taste. Cook until fragrant, 2-4 minutes. Set aside.

Once the timer goes off on the Instant Pot, let sit for at least 10 minutes; the pressure will release naturally. Then switch the Pressure Release to Venting to allow any last steam out.

Remove the squash from the Instant Pot and use a fork to shred the flesh into spaghetti-like strands. Toss with the garlic sage oil, add salt and pepper to taste, and serve warm.

10-Minute Balsamic Roasted Beets

20 Minutes or Less
7 Ingredients or Less

Serves 6 as a side
Prep Time: 1 minute
Cook Time: 10 minutes

Ingredients
6 medium beets, unpeeled
3 tablespoons balsamic vinegar
2 tablespoons olive oil
Salt to taste
Pepper to taste

Directions
Wash the beets well and remove any leaves. Add 1 cup of water to the Instant Pot and place the trivet on top. Arrange the beets on the trivet.

Lock the lid and set the Pressure Release to Sealing. Select the Pressure Cook or Manual setting and set the cooking time to 10 minutes at high pressure.

Once the timer goes off, use a kitchen towel or oven mitts to protect your hand and move the Pressure Release knob to Venting to perform a quick pressure release.

Remove the beets, allow to cool, and peel. The skin should slip off easily. Slice the beets into rounds or chop them into bite-sized pieces. Dress them with the balsamic vinegar, olive oil, and salt and pepper to taste.

Serve immediately or allow to marinate for 30 minutes for more flavor.

Flavor Bomb Asian Brussels Sprouts

20 Minutes or Less

Serves 4
Prep Time: 5 minutes
Cook Time: 3 minutes

Ingredients
1 tablespoon chopped almonds
¾ cup vegetable broth
3 tablespoons coconut aminos
1 tablespoon rice wine vinegar
2 tablespoons sesame oil
1 teaspoon crushed red pepper flakes
2 teaspoons garlic powder
1 teaspoon onion powder
1 tablespoon paprika
¼ teaspoon cayenne pepper
1 teaspoon salt
2 lbs. Brussels sprouts, halved

Directions
Select the Sauté setting and add the almonds. Stir constantly until toasted, watching them carefully so they don't burn. Press Cancel to turn off the Sauté setting.

In a medium bowl, combine all remaining ingredients except for the Brussels sprouts. Add the sauce to the Instant Pot along with the Brussels sprouts. Stir well to coat the Brussels in sauce.

Lock the lid and set the Pressure Release to Sealing. Select the Pressure Cook or Manual setting and set the cooking time to 3 minutes at high pressure.

Once the timer goes off, use a kitchen towel or oven mitts to protect your hand and move the Pressure Release knob to Venting to perform a quick pressure release.

Open the lid and taste, adding salt and pepper to taste, if necessary. Serve warm over cauliflower rice or as a side for a protein.

Note: For spicier Brussels sprouts, try doubling or tripling the quantity of cayenne pepper, or add a few tablespoons of your favorite Whole Foods compliant hot sauce.

Amazingly Adaptable Roasted Potatoes

Kid-Friendly
7 Ingredients or Less
20 Minutes or Less

Serves 8
Prep Time: 5 minutes
Cook Time: 7 minutes

Ingredients
¼ cup olive oil or ghee
1½ lbs. russet potatoes, peeled or unpeeled, in 1-inch pieces
1 teaspoon garlic powder
1 teaspoon sea salt
¼ teaspoon pepper
1 cup chicken broth

Directions
Select the Sauté setting on the Instant Pot and heat the olive oil or ghee. Add the potatoes, salt, pepper, and garlic powder to the pot and sauté for 5 minutes, stirring constantly. Add the chicken broth and stir well.

Press Cancel to reset the cooking method. Lock the lid and set the Pressure Release to Sealing. Select the Pressure Cook or Manual setting and set the cooking time to 7 minutes at high pressure.

Once the timer goes off, use a kitchen towel or oven mitts to protect your hand and move the Pressure Release knob to Venting to perform a quick pressure release.

Open the lid and taste, adding salt and pepper to taste, if necessary. Serve warm over a salad or as a side for chicken or another protein.

Note: This recipe can be adapted many ways, according to your family's tastes. Try adding a favorite spice mix, curry powder, or cayenne pepper before pressure cooking, fresh herbs like rosemary and thyme after cooking, or a drizzle of truffle oil before serving.

Garlicky Mashed Potatoes

Kid-Friendly
7 Ingredients or Less
20 Minutes or Less

Serves 4
Prep Time: 5 minutes
Cook Time: 8 minutes

Ingredients
4 medium potatoes, peeled and cut into 1-inch chunks
1 cup vegetable broth
6 cloves garlic, peeled and halved
½ cup unsweetened original almond milk
1 tablespoon garlic powder
3 tablespoons ghee
Salt to taste
Optional: 1 tablespoon chopped parsley for serving

Directions
In the Instant Pot, add the potatoes, broth, and garlic. Lock the lid and set the Pressure Release to Sealing. Select the Pressure Cook or Manual setting and set the cooking time to 8 minutes at high pressure.

Once the timer goes off, use a kitchen towel or oven mitts to protect your hand and move the Pressure Release knob to Venting to perform a quick pressure release.

Open the Instant Pot and mash the potatoes using a potato masher, immersion blender, or fork. Stir in the almond milk, garlic powder, and ghee, and add salt and pepper to taste.

Serve warm and sprinkle with fresh parsley, if desired.

Easiest Baked Sweet Potatoes

Kid-Friendly
7 Ingredients or Less

Serves 4
Prep Time: 1 minute
Cook Time: 20 minutes

Ingredients
4 medium sweet potatoes

Directions
Place the Instant Pot trivet inside the pot. Prick the potatoes all over with a fork to allow them to vent. Arrange potatoes in one layer on top of the trivet and add 1 cup of water to the pot.

Lock the lid and set the Pressure Release to Sealing. Select the Steam setting and set the cooking time to 20 minutes at high pressure.

Once the timer goes off, let sit for at least 10 minutes; the pressure will release naturally. Then switch the Pressure Release to Venting to allow any last steam out.

Note: You can use this same method for regular potatoes.

Balsamic and Garlic Stewed Kale

20 Minutes or Less
7 Ingredients or Less

Serves 4 as a side
Prep Time: 5 minutes
Cook Time: 4 minutes

Ingredients
1 tablespoon olive oil
5 cloves garlic, roughly chopped
2 large bunches kale, de-stemmed and roughly chopped
1 cup chicken broth
Salt to taste
Pepper to taste
3 tablespoons balsamic vinegar
1/8 teaspoon crushed red pepper flakes (Or omit, if you don't like spicy food.)

Directions
Select the Sauté setting and heat the olive oil. Add the garlic and cook, stirring constantly, until fragrant, 3-5 minutes. Add the kale, broth, and salt and pepper to taste.

Press Cancel to reset the cooking method. Lock the lid and set the Pressure Release to Sealing. Select the Pressure Cook or Manual setting and set the cooking time to 4 minutes at high pressure.

Once the timer goes off, use a kitchen towel or oven mitts to protect your hand and move the Pressure Release knob to Venting to perform a quick pressure release.

Open the lid and add the balsamic vinegar and crushed red pepper flakes, if using. Taste and add more salt and pepper if necessary. Serve warm.

Whole Foods Compliant Sauces and Seasonings

Homemade BBQ Sauce

Kid-Friendly
20 Minutes or Less

Makes 2 cups
Prep Time: 0 Minutes
Cook Time: 10 Minutes

½ cup unsweetened apple juice
¼ cup tomato paste
1 teaspoon garlic powder
1 teaspoon onion powder
1 teaspoon paprika
¼ teaspoon cayenne pepper (Or ½ teaspoon, if you like spicy BBQ sauce.)
½ teaspoon salt
2 tablespoons apple cider vinegar
Optional: 1 teaspoon liquid smoke

Select the Sauté setting on the Instant Pot. Add all of the ingredients and stir well. Allow to cook for at least 10 minutes, until thickened. Taste and adjust salt or spice level to your taste.

Ladle the sauce into food-safe containers and store in the refrigerator. Or, to use the BBQ sauce right away, add chicken, beef, or other ingredients to the Instant Pot and follow the manufacturer's recommended cooking times and pressure setting.

Note: This barbeque sauce will be less sweet than you might be used to, because it has no added sugar. To add more sweetness, you can puree 5 pitted dates in a food processor with a bit of water and incorporate into the sauce.

Whole Foods Compliant Lemon Pepper Seasoning

Kid-Friendly
7 Ingredients or Less
20 Minutes or Less

Prep Time: 5 Minutes
Cook Time: 0 minutes

Ingredients
6 lemons, zested
2 teaspoons garlic powder
1 tablespoon freshly cracked black pepper
2 teaspoons salt

In a small bowl, combine all ingredients. Store in a tight-sealing container in the refrigerator and use on chicken, fish, potatoes, and vegetables.

Whole Foods Compliant Taco Seasoning

Kid-Friendly
7 Ingredients or Less
20 Minutes or Less

Prep Time: 2 Minutes
Cook Time: 0 minutes

Ingredients
2 tablespoons chili powder
1½ tablespoons ground cumin
2 teaspoons garlic powder
¼ teaspoon cayenne pepper, or to taste
1 teaspoon dried oregano
2 teaspoons salt
1 teaspoon black pepper

In a small bowl, combine all ingredients. Store in a tight-sealing container at room temperature and use on chicken, fish, meat, potatoes, and vegetables.

Whole Foods Compliant Italian Seasoning

Kid-Friendly
7 Ingredients or Less
20 Minutes or Less

Prep Time: 2 Minutes
Cook Time: 0 minutes

Ingredients
1 tablespoon garlic powder
½ tablespoon dried oregano
½ teaspoon crushed red pepper flakes
1 teaspoon dried basil
1 teaspoon dried thyme
1 teaspoon salt
1 teaspoon black pepper

In a small bowl, combine all ingredients. Store in a tight-sealing container at room temperature and use on chicken, fish, meat, potatoes, and vegetables.

You can also make a delicious Italian dressing by adding olive oil and apple cider vinegar to this seasoning and shaking well. This makes a healthy, additive-free, sugar-free Italian dressing that can be used to marinate chicken, fish, and pork or can be drizzled over roasted vegetables.

Whole Foods Compliant Indian Spice Mix

Kid-Friendly
7 Ingredients or Less
20 Minutes or Less

Prep Time: 2 Minutes
Cook Time: 0 minutes

Ingredients
2 tablespoons curry powder
2 tablespoons cumin
2 teaspoons turmeric
2 teaspoons ground coriander
1 teaspoon ground ginger
½ teaspoon cinnamon

In a small bowl, combine all ingredients. Store in a tight-sealing container at room temperature and use on in curries or on chicken, fish, meat, potatoes, and vegetables.

Cooking Times for the Instant Pot Electric Pressure Cooker

Although certain foods like grains and beans aren't allowed on the most popular 30-day whole food diets, I wanted to include their suggested cooking times here anyway, should you ever need them for feeding fussy family members or entertaining.

In fact, the Instant Pot is a miracle worker for feeding family members who aren't doing the 30 Day Whole Foods Challenge. In just a few minutes, you can cook up nearly a week's worth of rice, quinoa, black beans, lentils, or other meal-building staples, so that your family can still eat the things they enjoy, even while you opt out (from both eating them *and* cooking them nightly!).

Keep these times handy for anytime you need a simple staple ingredient done quickly.

A note on cooking beans and other legumes in the Instant Pot:
Dried beans will double in volume after cooking, so never fill your electric pressure cooker more than halfway and be sure to fully cover the beans with liquid.

Dried Beans, Legumes, and Lentils	DRY Cooking Time (minutes)	SOAKED Cooking Time (minutes)
Black beans	20 – 25	6 – 8
Black-eyed peas	10 – 15	4 – 5
Chickpeas	35 – 40	10 – 15
Cannellini beans	30 – 35	8 – 10
Great Northern beans	25 – 30	8 – 10
Kidney beans, red	25 – 30	8 – 10
Kidney beans, white / Cannellini	30 – 35	8 – 10
Lentils, green	10 – 12	n/a
Lentils, brown	10 – 12	n/a
Lentils, red, split	5 – 6	n/a
Lentils, yellow, split (moong dal)	18 – 20	n/a

Lima beans	12 – 14	8 – 10
Navy beans	20 – 25	7 – 8
Pinto beans	25 – 30	8 – 10
Peas	6 – 10	n/a

Meat	Cooking Time (mins)
Beef, stew meat	20 / 450 gm / 1 lb
Beef, meatballs	8-10 / 450 gm / 1 lb
Beef (pot roast, steak, rump, round, chuck, blade or brisket), small pieces	15 / 450 gm / 1 lb
Beef (pot roast, steak, rump, round, chuck, blade or brisket), large pieces	20 / 450 gm / 1 lb
Beef, ribs	20 – 25
Beef, shanks	25 – 30
Chicken, breasts (boneless)	6 – 8
Chicken, whole 2-2.5 Kg	8 / 450 gm / 1 lb
Chicken, cut with bones	10 – 15
Chicken, bone stock	40 – 45
Ham, slices	9 – 12
Ham, picnic shoulder	8 / 450 gm / 1 lb
Lamb, cubes	10 – 15
Lamb, stew meat	12 – 15
Lamb, leg	15 / 450 gm / 1 lb

Pork, loin roast	20 / 450 gm / 1 lb
Pork, butt roast	15 / 450 gm / 1 lb
Pork, ribs	15 – 20
Turkey, breast (boneless)	7 – 9
Turkey, breast (whole)	20 – 25
Turkey, drumsticks (leg)	15 – 20
Veal, chops	5 – 8
Veal, roast	12 / 450 gm / 1 lb

Guidelines for Buying Organic Produce and Whole Foods

Buying organic can be expensive, but we all want to feed our families the healthiest and safest fruits and vegetables. That's where the Dirty Dozen and Clean Fifteen come in.

Each year, the Environmental Working Group issues its Shopper's Guide to Pesticides in Produce, which ranks the pesticide contamination of popular fruits and vegetables. Rankings are based on data from more than 35,200 samples which are tested each year by the U.S. Department of Agriculture and the Food and Drug Administration.

The top 15 types of produce that have the least amount of pesticide residue are known as the Clean Fifteen, while the top 12 most contaminated fruits and vegetables are called the Dirty Dozen.

By knowing which fruits and vegetables contain more pesticides and which contain less, you can make more informed choices and stretch your grocery dollar further.

The Dirty Dozen
When possible, buy these organic.

1. Strawberries
2. Spinach
3. Nectarines
4. Apples
5. Peaches
6. Pears
7. Cherries
8. Grapes
9. Celery
10. Tomatoes
11. Sweet bell peppers
12. Potatoes

The Clean Fifteen
These do not need to be bought organic.

1. Sweet Corn
2. Avocados
3. Pineapples
4. Cabbage
5. Onions
6. Sweet peas
7. Papayas
8. Asparagus
9. Mangos
10. Eggplant

11. Honeydew Melon
12. Kiwi
13. Cantaloupe
14. Cauliflower
15. Grapefruit

Metric Conversion Charts

If you use metric measurements in your cooking, use these handy charts to convert the recipes in this book to work in your kitchen. You can also find free and easy-to-use metric conversion calculators online.

1/4 tsp	= 1 ml		
1/2 tsp	= 2 ml		
1 tsp	= 5 ml		
3 tsp	= 1 tbl	= 1/2 fl oz	= 15 ml
2 tbls	= 1/8 cup	= 1 fl oz	= 30 ml
4 tbls	= 1/4 cup	= 2 fl oz	= 60 ml
5 1/3 tbls	= 1/3 cup	= 3 fl oz	= 80 ml
8 tbls	= 1/2 cup	= 4 fl oz	= 120 ml
10 2/3	= 2/3 cup	= 5 fl oz	= 160 ml
12 tbls	= 3/4 cup	= 6 fl oz	= 180 ml
16 tbls	= 1 cup	= 8 fl oz	= 240 ml
1 pt	= 2 cups	= 16 fl oz	= 480 ml
1 qt	= 4 cups	= 32 fl oz	= 960 ml

	33 fl oz	= 1000 ml	= 1 l

Freeze Water	32° F	0° C	
Room Temp.	68° F	20° C	
Boil Water	212° F	100° C	
Bake	325° F	160° C	3
	350° F	180° C	4
	375° F	190° C	5
	400° F	200° C	6
	425° F	220° C	7
	450° F	230° C	8

Helpful Resources

If you'd like to learn more about the Whole Foods 30-day diet and the Instant Pot, I highly recommend these books:

The Essential Instant Pot Cookbook: Fresh and Foolproof Recipes for Your Electric Pressure Cooker by Coco Morante

Dinner in an Instant: 75 Modern Recipes for Your Pressure Cooker, Multicooker, and Instant Pot by Melissa Clark

It Starts With Food: Discover the Whole30 and Change Your Life in Unexpected Ways by Dallas Hartwig and Melissa Hartwig

The Whole30: The 30-Day Guide to Total Health and Food Freedom: Dallas Hartwig and Melissa Hartwig

Did you find these recipes helpful?

If so, would you consider paying it forward

by leaving a review on Amazon?

A review is the best way to help out an author, and hopefully it will help the next person find their way to healthier, easier Whole Foods Instant Pot meals, too!

To leave a review:

Type this link into your browser: http://bit.ly/WholeInstantPot

OR

Google search "whole foods instant pot cookbook Emily Othan" and click the first link.

This should take you to the book page, where you can leave a review.

Thank you so much!

Gift a book = give a meal!

We believe everybody deserves a warm, healthy meal to come home to. That's why we've committed to donating one meal to a family in need through Feeding America for each copy sold of this book. So just by purchasing a copy of this book, you've helped feed a neighbor in need—thank you so much for that.

To spread the love, gift a copy of this book to a friend. They'll love you for it, and you'll be making a difference in another family's life!

To gift a book:

Type this link into your browser: http://bit.ly/WholeInstantPot

OR

Google search "whole foods instant pot cookbook Emily Othan" and click the first link. This should take you to the book page, where you can leave a review.

This should take you to the book page, where on the right, you'll see a button that says "Give as a Gift."

Happy gifting!

Made in the USA
Middletown, DE
04 April 2019